THE BAT HAD BLUE EYES

For ANNE,
Toank for you
for your close
listening!
My BEST,
Betsy
July 30, '93
Launch

The Bat Had Blue Eyes

Betsy Warland

women's
PRESS

CANADIAN CATALOGUING IN PUBLICATION DATA
Warland, Betsy, 1946—
      The bat had blue eyes
(Not a luxury poetry series)
Poems.
ISBN 0-88961-184-X

1. Adult child sexual abuse victims – Poetry.
I. Title.

PS8595.A7745B38 1993   C811´.54   C93-094017-2
PR9199.3.W364B38   1993

Copy editor: Angela Hryniuk
Cover design: Sandra Haar
Cover illustration: Copyright © 1993 Yolanda Van Dyck from the
painting "I'm telling anyway."

This book was produced by the collective effort of Women's Press.
Women's Press gratefully acknowledges the financial support of the
Canada Council and the Ontario Arts Council.

Printed and bound in Canada
1 2 3 4 5   1997 1996 1995 1994 1993

For Joyce Frazee

To those who companioned me in the writing and revising — Daphne Marlatt, Steven Warland, Di Brandt, Angela Hryniuk, Sandy Duncan, Stan Dragland, Cheryl Sourkes, Yolanda Van Dyck, Vivienne Spiteri, Jeannie Lochrie, Sue Astley, Patsy Ludwick, Kerry Sandomirsky, Christina Jastrzembska — thank you each and all. I also wish to thank Matthew Coleman, and my sangha, as well as The Banff Centre, Leighton Artist Colony, for providing the ideal healing and working space in which I began writing this manuscript.

The script, *The Bat Had Blue Eyes* was first performed at the Women in View 1993 Festival and can be obtained from the author via Women's Press.

i.

family secrets

0 characters
a story obscured
a girl invisible
a woman haunted
a writer's work:

                              in-the-visible

this time there are witnesses

zero characters

                whistle flows

around mountains

                soothing?

         secretive?

                who is there going where?

zer(0) character intolerable

words —

         frantic claw marks

against the blankness

I clings
to anything
that will support its weight

I subject to
gravity of suffering

memory a jealous lover

words will not
leave me alone

if i tell this old story
in some new way
will it let me go?

will words become bored,
abandon me
for another desperate one?

i've read if you play dead
the bear may sniff you
then amble away

Memory is most true when not translated into words.
A smell or taste, long forgotten then remembered —
sensation so vivid, stories so intact, they shock us.

With words we begin our forgetting. Tongue forgets
taste, forgets touch, as it quickens to its work of
words.

Words that force forgetting: memories then held in our
senses, speaking through symptoms, nervous physical
habits, inexplicable intuitions, redundant emotional
culs-de-sac.

To remember, we rely on words, words already a
substitute for the experience we seek to call up.
Memory saved in senses translated into language:
re/storing, remembering, re-storying.

Words to remember what we had no words for —
suffering frequently endemic to these experiences.

Sudden pungent smell of semen on the web of my
hand, so strong, precise, my therapist recognized it too.

hands never still

you notice
if you know what to look for

hand me down
how many generations?

her thumb rubs 'round
side of curved index finger
'round around
                        or
incessantly
over tips of fingers
little finger up to index
trying to wipe
                        something off
i pick
tear
bits of skin off
endlessly
surreptitiously
(hoping no one will notice
the little gouges)

he puts his watch on
takes it off
on off
on off
pacing
winding
it winding it

unlike the others
his working hands were gloved,
surprisingly soft

these hands have been places
they wish they hadn't been

hands down
nobody wins
in this game

heavy hand
sleight of hand
no body

It began when my parents hired a "cleaning lady."
The house the self; Mrs. Barnett the stranger. My
mother started to hide her valuables. After awhile it
was difficult to recall where she had hidden every-
thing. Accusations of stealing then began. On the
surface, she remained congenial. Her paranoia poured
out only to us. When any one of us happened upon
the missing letter opener, the Porsgrund plate or the
Norwegian broach my mother would insist Mrs.
Barnett had put it there. When we would assert that it
had been there all along — that she had simply
forgotten where it was hidden — my mother flared
with indignation. I confronted my father about it.
"You've got to stop this, Mrs. Barnett isn't taking
anything and you know it." He refused to discuss the
matter. His lifelong protectiveness of my mother
precluded any criticism.

My mother's hiding, losing and accusing cycle turned
in an ever-deepening spiral. Over the years several
women were eventually fired in an emotional,
religiously-inspired confrontation. When my father
died my mother was forced to give up the house. She
was too fearful to spend a night alone. When we
returned to close it up the apparent worth of every
object had to be questioned: the lid of an empty
hair-spray can might contain a precious ring. All the
objects that had been "stolen" were found. As we
reported these findings to her the response was
always, "Oh, she felt guilty and brought it back."

In the retirement home my mother's cycle spun faster and deeper. She began to leave accusatory notes for the staff housekeeper at the sites of various hiding spots which had been found and pillaged. Because her valuables were far fewer in the tiny apartment, she hid objects which were closer to home: her raincap, earrings, stockings, and undergarments. More and more of her time was consumed with hiding, losing, hunting, accusing. She became afraid of leaving her room or sleeping at night because this was when "that woman" would steal in. Eventually she was moved into the extended care section where residents are allowed minimal belongings. We all heaved a sigh of relief. She was initially placed in a double room and chose to remain there when a single became available. Even now she complains about her roommate (under whose mattress she hides her purse) but feels safer not being in a room alone.

Like everyone else, I have reasoned with her, tried to understand, ignored, distracted, reassured and threatened her. "They could sue you if you don't have proof." None of it has made any difference.

Recently, during a highly charged emotional confrontation with my younger brother, my mother confessed to being a victim of incest. When he told me I had a shock of recognition. It was one of her most beloved ones who had invaded her, taken her valuables, left her spinning in shame and terror. Her senseless behaviour suddenly made sense.

i thought
i was the only one —

My mother and I are unlikely to ever speak of one of
the most important things we share. Words would fail
us miserably. What we are instinctively remembering
is who we each were before the spinning, before the
gouging.

memory
the scene of an accident
everyone has a different version
adjustments must be made
to eradicate contra/dictions
or (else)

        antagonisms set in

              "I don't dwell in the past."
              he doesn't remember

he can't remember

(like father)
he told himself
he was just making certain
she fell asleep

              (like son)
              he told her
              it was "just a game"

just.

is it any wonder
words confounded her?

he willed her not to notice

              he told me "*forget* it."

0 characters?
no story.

First, learn the preliminaries.
Think that all phenomena are like dreams.

from *A Direct Path To Enlightenment*

i'm in my bedroom in our old house. my cousin is
staying with us and has been sleeping with me in my
bed. when i get up i notice that she has left her clothes
strewn all over the floor. the bed sheets and covers
have also been left in disarray. i'm hurrying to get
ready for school but know i have to tidy up my room
before i leave. while i'm untangling the bedclothes i
notice a large, orangeish-coloured daddy long legs. i
brush it off, half intending to kill it, but miss it. it is
very determined to stay where it is. i decide i have to
kill it. i can't bear the thought of making my bed with
it still in there. as i strike its head falls off. its body
reacts with intense violence, emitting several angry,
nuclear-like explosions of little eggs which are white
and wrapped in a fine filament. i realize these are
baby spiders which will hatch momentarily. i'm
frightened by the hundreds of eggs everywhere and
unnerved that my intention of killing the spider,
which i thought would stop the situation, has made it
much worse. i've only a few minutes to pick up the
eggs before they hatch and begin crawling all over my
room. i run out for help: no one. when i return i find
Mrs. Barnett dropping minute tapioca-size moth balls
all over the floor but i'm afraid this won't work fast
enough. i fetch the vacuum cleaner and begin sucking
eggs up with the hose. my mattress and bedding are
all that remain in the profusion of white.

rockabye baby...
rockabye baby...
        getting his off

bedrock
rock bottom

mons veneris mons veneris mons veneris
o vulnerable *mountain* mons mountain mons
mountains
o luminous ring o disk o halo of
rock reflected light
giant cradle holding
me of the many generations
who came out of the mountains
of a northern country shaped like a spoon
o mons veneris mons veneris o venerable mountains
this was not about spooning this was not
o rock us in your ancient arms
it is
me of the many generations
i have caught a glimpse of
the fabulous motion
                        your *paramount* waves
nothing forgotten

                        only forgiven
it is said you cannot move a mountain
matter ever changing

a woman writing in public
absorbed in words
unaware of others
occasionally
running her fingers through her hair
or tossing it back
occasionally
retreating from
the intensity of
staring at anything
not demanding her attention
but words soon want her again
a woman alone
in public
unconcerned with others
making her own text
in public
not letters or post cards
but words so urgent she must stop
like a rock
give herself to them
as we flow around her

ii.

photographs

Finally we're shown the door, and we try to take consolation in the oblivion which people call memory.

from The Quest For Christa T.

standing there
small back to the camera

some mountain somewhere in Colorado
mom insisted dad photograph
behind me

standing there
defiant back

i didn't want to
didn't want to pretend

                                        snap shot

ringing in my ears
family joke for years

was she crying?
she doesn't remember.

what had pushed her to this point?
she doesn't remember

the only testimony
her hanging head

to curl up like a caterpillar

vain attempt

home in the green mountains
sea mountains becoming islands
on the endless slope to

                                water-reflected light

mountains

on the edge of
less dramatic
more a part of

shape-changers

                       every few feet

you wonder
who they are again

i forgot how to read in grade 3.

At the time, the explanation was that I had been taken out of our town school and placed in a one-room country school which had a poor teacher. Miss Rosemore was "a Bible thumper" who little understood the temporal world of children. She lacked heart (she'd rather be reading the Bible), and discipline (she'd rather be reading the Bible, *alone*).

This was my first encounter with chaos and anarchy. The other seasoned students were relentless in their undermining of her irritable and tenuous authority. Recess was 'war.' During class time, I retreated, taught myself how to draw — a form of reading I could trust.

there's another reason i forgot how to read in grade 3.

A reason that shook my faith in the written word far more profoundly. I was being sexually abused. As is nearly always the case, my abuse was unacknow-ledged. Invisible. And, as is often the case, my abusers' words placed the blame on me.

Read. ar-; To fit together. Old English raeden, to advise: READ; REDE, raeden, condition: HATRED, KINDRED.

Although we weren't Bible thumpers my family was a religious one. My parents were the "pillars of the church." We were raised to believe that when we rebelled or simply disagreed with their opinions we were disobeying "God Himself."

The written word **was** The Bible — The Law: one in the same. The Word was The Truth. No questions asked.

in grade 3 i lost faith in words.

At 43 I understood why.

Faith, Latin fides, perhaps explicable by qui per fidem decipit, (he) who deceives by means of faith or trust.

grandma and i are looking into the camera. our faces are open with an almost fierce delight. grandma is sitting with her large hand resting on the saucer beneath the cup of coffee. i'm standing on her other side, arm resting on the back of the chair, around her shoulders. our heads are nearly at the same level. our smiles self-possessed. a round angel food birthday cake is in front of us on the table (our birthdays 9 days apart). in the window behind us the flash bulb's reflection has made a mysterious, soft ball of light above grandma's head. like an aura, like a solid halo. grandma's wearing the snowflake broach over her heart. the flash against her dark dress makes it glow. coming across this photograph after many years, the obvious solidarity stunned me. the pleasure in each other's company. this was the one person i had trusted.

Simone de Beauvoir believed that once a memory was transposed into writing, the original memory was replaced and forgotten. Marguerite Duras writes similarly that the process of taking a photograph "promotes forgetting."

Memory transposed into a textual or visual image is framed. It relinquishes the mutability it might have enjoyed within the shiftings of our mind and the minds of others sharing the original experience. Its chatter and argument no longer mutable, but mute.

tick-tock
knock on rock

bodies in line
bodies in repetitive configurations
year after year
smile squint
context the pretext
where & when increasingly forgotten
even the cast
                              "Who's that?"
never satiated with the sight of ourselves
until we began to leave
shrink away
in ourselves
from ourselves
from one another
our bodies' focus falters
skin becomes transparent
we bring the camera out of habit, in case
it often remains
as bodies disappear
one by one
from the line

a table heaped with 90 years of photographs. we're to destroy every one. the sound of five scissors. a life rendered into pieces. the old woman upstairs is on the verge of dying. when the last photograph is cut up, scissors put down, she will pass through. an oval table. no words. only metal through paper. she wants to slip into that dark corridor — the light intense at the end. hurry. finally a mountain of pieces. i tell her. she says no, something is still preventing her: there must be more somewhere. we are certain we've destroyed them all. she insists. turn the house inside out. then between two walls i find an album of her grade school class photographs. bladed hands destroy every last one. i run to tell her. she has already passed through. her whimsical smile — her wave good-bye.

a life
no longer posed
framed
a life no longer
documented
doctor(ed)

as my grandmother's namesake
i was promised the
wide gold band
turning on her
knotty finger
                    good hand
the stroke had not marred
with which she held
or pinched
with enraged in/validism

bed*ridden, rida, rider*

powerful woman
i remember prone
her language
out of focus

when she died
my mother maintained
i was too young
wore the band
on her thinning hand

o luminous ring o disk o halo
down the drain

       after supper
my mother cleaning up
food scraps
running water
flick of the switch —
i can still hear that sound

                           metal mashing metal

to write
back to the camera
to write outside
the viewfinder
be shadow & light

                     ever changing

not black & white

photo, light + graph, to write
in night's

          half-light

          familiar shapes

               fantastical

fireflies' errant punctuation

                          o endless sentence

moving hand in dark
my fleeting name

               in sparkler script

iii.

heart lines

warm & heavy in solitary sleep
screams shaking me awake
claws between breasts
menacing glare
black wings
width
of my trembling

> mons mountains
> mons pubis
> mons veneris

at the side of my bed
under the cover of night
he came
> skins rubbing
> (o mons pubis)

> > beneath a sheet cold as snow…

vampire *bat*
so apt
at blood sucking
> "Now I lay me down to sleep,
> I pray the Lord my soul to keep…"

its sleeping prey
rarely aware of its activities
(vibrating shadow on my right)

> Pater of the night.

out of character
or in character?

nobody would ever imagine —

precisely.

        no body.

now i know
the least likely
the most likely

the plot
chip off the old block

When one whom I have benefitted with great hope
 Unreasonably hurts me very badly.
 I will learn to view that person
 As an excellent spiritual guide.

  from "The Eight Stanzas for Training the Mind"

0:

"cipher"

"nonentity"

"a method of transforming a text in order to conceal its meaning"

"a sight setting that enables a firearm to shoot on target"

"nobody"

"the lowest point or point of origin"

"absent, inoperative, or irrelevant in specified circumstances: zero gravity"

character:

"a graphic symbol used in writing & printing"

"a magical emblem"

"moral or ethical strength"

"the complex of mental & ethical traits marking & often individualizing a person, group, or nation"

"a person portrayed in a drama, novel, or other artistic piece"

nostalgia for narrative
credo of characters
everything spelled out

            finite finis

to survive the endings endlessly

             o sweet embrace

             I clings
             to anything
             that will support its weight

stored
story

there are always reasons

when characterized
will they *matter* no more,
mother no more?

mirror, smei-, mirus, mirage
words will not leave us
alone

                              a stage
the infant notices the mirror
secures the gaze
assumes the reflected image
                      birthing herself

into separateness
a life of characters

language the great magician

saws us in half
(only an illusion)

Ladies & Gentlemen,
are you prepared to see
life is more
than what meets the eye?

then, opens the box —
(it was just your imagination)

Ladies & Gentlemen,
may I present to you
Madame Remarkable — perfectly w/hole!

words are no mother
hold no loyalties
mean
different things
in different mouths
amenable to anyone who calls their name
willingly at the service of truths
or lies

one of the few incidents they remember about my
childhood is the time i ran away. spring. after the
great black fields had been plowed, they lay like
moonless nights around us. a little girl, 4 or 5
perhaps. no one noticed my absence. when i returned
exhausted from the up and down of deep furrows, i
blurted out in tearful frustration "my feet were so
busy, busy, busy!" the punch line everyone always
laughed at. it doesn't occur to me, until 35 years later,
to wonder why i ran away; to wonder about the
missing parts of the story which no one recalls. now i
can remember my feelings of humilation, anger,
hopelessness as my legs struggled to run across the
frowns on the earth. no context. i too have laughed all
these years; have told the story, that isn't a story but a
punch line, myself. gradually i have remembered
other things — how unsafe i felt in the house, how i'd
do anything to escape, going further and further
afield: to the barn, the out-buildings, the woods, the
dredge ditch, the river two miles away.

solitary.
       on the run.

a girl of 4 or 5
'til she is 45

Framed: a method for getting rid of the competition.

words are for
forgetting

the dog lives for stick chewing, chasing, fetching
his body flies over earth
swims icy-green water makes magnificent leaps
ivory body taut, radiating
the dog knows many words "use your nose" "this way"
only part of his vocabulary
yet the dog prefers the language of hands

This is about memory. A kind of memory that a great many of us have fiercely repressed. A kind of memory which we have no awareness of. Which profoundly shapes our intimate lives without our understanding. Without our assent. It has no relationship to formal education or 'remember when....' This memory is the interface (inner face) of a self-induced amnesia.

from *Proper Deafinitions*

re-membering
dismembered pieces of memory

re-learning how to read
shapes of words
like shapes of pieces

edges my only guide

there are those who say
"Why dig around?"
"Is this literature?"
"Some things are best left unsaid."

*(doubt, dubitare, to waiver, vibrate
didumos, double, testicles)*

before bat was —

                              beetle, bitan, to bite
inexplicable horror of…
its sound beneath my bed
how i'd yell for him to
come
                in the night
                                take it away!
                black June bug
                that whirring, flailing sound

next to my ear —
years later in our bed
my lover's thumb idly rubbing
                        side of index finger
terror erupting like a sudden injection of
                                his lingering silhouette

that sound

as she writes
she looks out on
water-reflected light
eyes squint
in contrast to monitor's dark screen

fir & alder
reeds for the wind

the shape of the lake —
a heart
                in the rock in the sea
                                island mountain

she writes
at the heart's cleavage

where it clefts or
                splits apart

iv.

little screams

To become oneself, with all one's strength.

Difficult.

A bomb, a speech, a rifle shot — and the world can look a different place. And then where is this 'self'?

from The Quest For Christa T.

my 92 year old aunt
refuses death
refuses food
refuses language

speaks her will
through the grip of her hand —
to be wheeled up & down the hallway endlessly

kept alive without a life

i barely recognize her
she doesn't remember me

when i lean to say goodbye
she says with wonderment: "eyes"

                      that blue
                      our history

they say men die of broken hearts. my father's first heart attack. in hospital. night. his empty twin bed. my mother's steadiness disintegrates. "… as if 'fear' had never been anything but another word for death."[*] in other bedrooms we are sinking into the deep of exhausted sleep. her scream catapults us — we collide with her running down the hall. "there's a bat in our bedroom!" broom. pillow. empty ice cream bucket. finally my brother and i catch it. what to do. we want to set it free. she refuses, certain it will find its way back in. finally a compromise: we'll leave it outside beneath the upside-down bucket, outside, with a large rock on top. my mother adds a codicil, deftly lifts a side of the bucket and sprays it with insecticide. cruelty an act of cowardice? in the morning it is not dead. my father. we have to go. my mother resolute. my younger brother's job (handle it). can't bring himself to club it, step on it, besides, it might fly away. digs small hole, slides bat quickly in, grabs fists of soil. little screams. he hadn't expected that. little screams 'til the cool earth silences it. he tells me the story, imitates its sound. we laugh with relief and nervousness. death unearths a bizarre sense of humour. years later he can still hear its cries.

---

[*] from *The Quest for Christa T.*

futile claws
at the cover of soil

bed, bhedh-, to dig.

not a bed of its making
but a place to lie

badjam, garden plot,
sleeping place

kept under cover
fears crop up

kill the symbol
hide the story

its screams
stifle our own

maintain illusion
of happy home

                    but

if bat were only bat,
to whose arms would story run?

Bat is ... rebirth ... Shaman death is
the symbolic death of the initiate
to the old ways of life and personal
identity ... the shaman-to-be is sent
to a certain location to dig his or
her grave and spend the night in
the womb of Mother Earth totally alone,
with the mouth of the grave covered
by a blanket.

from *Medicine Cards*

                              mons mountains
                              mons pubis
                              mons veneris

days later i realized
the bat had blue eyes

i knew them well
later i went to him:
"I remember. I know what happened."

each spoke their pain, agreed
not to meet this way again

he shrank to normal size
lowering his wings

eyes no longer menacing
yet troubled ... he had other destinations

                    our eyes —

"there is nothing more i can do."
(finally to say those words)

then he turned —
& the dusk sky received him

fogbound

ridge across the water
quiet again

deadly periods

days of
everything on edge

each shot
           caught her breath
often without consciousness
                         squealing brakes of a distant car
she waited for metal crash
impact/implosion
           next shot/echo

                     echoing

who hears the deer fall?

rifle, rifler, to cut a spiral groove

I call my mother. "I know just which one it is — it's the little one, she's so slick. Impresses everyone with how hard she works so they'd never suspect her. I'm going to tell her tomorrow I know what she's up to, I know it's her, and she better bring my dress back or I'll tell them."

story stuck
in its *groove*
grave, engraves

she looks at her hands
little red gouges

              picked at picked at

(pick, piccare, prick, pierce)

footsteps. she's home! he didn't expect her yet, doesn't answer her calls, hopes she'll think we're outdoors. footsteps. only a few seconds. "put on your pants." spot of blood (it wasn't because of riding horses). hiding in the storage room (not supposed to be in here). his name (he's supposed to be in charge), then anxiously — mine (he's supposed to be babysitting). footsteps up the stairs, stop at my door, his, then straight ahead. zippers. he grabs an old *Life* as she flings open the door. her eyes — mine (this is not a dream): everything in that look. me terrified she'll find out desperately wanting her to (please mom, can't you *see*?). she hesitates, glances away — then deletes. "why are you in here?" "just reading to Betsy" he says. and she believes him.

"...[the] wheel of suffering revolves again and again."

from *The Treasury of Knowledge*

v.

the letter

What I saw wasn't a continuous text to be sure, only a few notes, and I couldn't figure out the connections. After the curious sentence about the difficulty of saying 'I,' came the words: 'Facts! Stick to the facts.' And underneath, in brackets: *But what are the facts?*

from The Quest For Christa T.

fact, facere, to do, make, facies, shape, face

making face
losing face

face our i(d)entity

type cast
type/face

to be more
than a type/writer

everything was slow motion. one grain of sand on the packed down earth. countless generations of paws, feet, hooves coming down. i was to turn the grain, half a rotation at a time. painstaking. with each turn i could read the energy in the earth below, which contrary to what i'd been told, was profoundly vertical, highly specific. everything that had happened, deposited — essence utterly intact. sometimes the energies, from one half-rotation to the next, were similar. sometimes radically different, even contradictory. the exactness, the magnitude, fascinated me. frightened me.

A poet friend writes, "it's not just words that make experience/memory disappear, but the way we respond to pain and remembered pain differently, than to pleasure."

More motivated to recall pleasure than pain. Every time I was abused I didn't want to believe it. Doubted it. Told myself something nice was going to happen not something bad.

In this way I contributed to my forgetting.

How to reconcile remembering with forgetting: the i who knew she was being abused with the i who disowned me, pretended otherwise; the i made invisible by language and the i becoming visceral in words?

Can i relinquish an i not of my own making? Wouldn't that be more an act of giving in, not letting go?

Can i make I; beget I? Or is it a process of recognizing what's inherited; what choices we have in using our i material? Realizing, rematerializing, then (i)mmaterializing.

I-story: that first deep wound. A lifetime of variations, repetition as affirmation: "History repeats itself." A kind of disbelief. Making it happen over and over to remember unauthorized i-story. Inside that, the terror of not having i-story. Is there anything to see with a naked i?

Can i work with words and empty the mind of them? Can i learn to escape words' relentless tyranny and still be a writer? Still be. Calm abiding. Ego death — i's mind set at rest.

Femininity and the female body have taught i about the fluid nature of i. How relative and insubstantial i is. Without envy i watches the effort required by men to endlessly reassert, maintain, and defend their I. Terror of the disintegrating I.

I makes you, she, he, them, it.

I/deals
spending my whole life trying to catch my I.

I/strains
Ignores the I/sores of its own intolerance.

Can i write an i in the process of disinheriting itself,
an i that knows an i-full isn't the whole story, that
recognizes word as angel not servant?

i, yodh, hand.

No longer (i)dolizing words for actuality.
i-opener, finger pointing at moon —

not "moon"

to her cat it was obvious
you gingerly walk across

                              the keys
                                like coals
                (this was real belief)
or
simply lie down on words
for a nap
elemental
like rock
water
sun-warmed
earth

cat was puzzled by
her intense silences
vacant stares
sporadic staccato typing
possesive snatching up of paper
beneath his muddy paws

wasn't his purr perfect
didn't his fur smell of sweet earth
weren't poems a lovely place

to curl up & drift into

incest — quietly passed from generation to generation
until someone breaks the invisible chain.

"… it is me of the many generations…"

in my family — 7 generations, a healer said.

the part i left out of my bed dream: my mother
removing the furniture and bedframe while i'm out of
my room, replacing it with my great-great-great
grandfather's headboard.

brother — i have broken the chain.

7 years to say their names
11 years to write:

>   father.
>   brother.

before that —
30 years of nearly no sexual sensation

but an editor writes
"… the experience of abuse is shadowy
… almost assumed…"

twilight half-world
obliterated, ob, away from + littera, letter

twilight —

>   one dead.

half-world —

>   the other with no recall.

the perfect crime
no witnesses
no corroboration —
neither able to speak

who abused them?

>   i can not speak for them

imagine the details
i think it's safe
to assume you can

mergansers'
watery wakes write

              Vs on green-grey stillness

intersecting —

           make T, D, X, B

      sideways

          M & W

language quack of *consonants,*
consonare, to sound at the same time,
harmonize, agree

underwater dives
write their only vowel

               o-o-o-O-O-O-O-O

o rippling o

        luminous ring o

             disk o

                 halo of

No metaphor
Mountains ARE our mothers.

from *Dream On*

the first time i held her
she shrank in my arms
            (mother)
small as her tears
so little solace
so little shelter
            (mother)
the scare in her muscles
loosened its grip
            (mother)
she rested a moment
                        like a lung after heaving
a long-held sigh

we weren't afraid

i no longer resented
the mothering she never gave,
namesake for her mother
who couldn't give it either

her long-held hope:
                        the name
                        her pain

around & around
        we have been
countless times
           taking our turns
      mothering

My friend writes, "i'm thinking of Kristeva's *Desire In Language*, for example — how the body seeks to find expression in language, not in order to be erased by it, but to be spoken, right back to the erotic, unmediated pleasures of the baby self."

her mirage — words

Unlike my friend, who was abused before she had language, my abusers used words to secure my silence.

which was my forgetting. mi rage.

my mirage — no words

(mother)
i have held her in the circle of my arms
i have passed through

        the O of her flesh
    through

        his zero of forgetting
to hold & be held
weightless in the curve of

        o luminous ring o

            disk o

             halo of

to remember this
oh!

how my lover,
a lover of words,
renders me speechless
drives me down to earth's opening sound

oooOOOOOO

& i let her o let/her
return me to
mother letter

Sources Quoted

A Direct Path To Enlightenment, 'Jam-mGon Kong-sPrul, Kagyukunkhyab Chuling.

A Very Easy Death, Simone de Beauvoir, Pantheon Books.

Dream On, Chrystos, Press Gang Publishers.

Medicine Cards, Jamie Sams & David Carson, Bear & Company.

Personal letter from poet Di Brandt.

Practicalities, Marguerite Duras, Grove Weidenfeld.

Proper Deafinitions, Betsy Warland, Press Gang Publishers.

The American Heritage Dictionary, Houghton Mifflin Company.

"The Eight Stanzas for Training the Mind" can be found in *Kindness, Clarity and Insight*, The Fourteenth Dalai Lama, Snow Lion Publications.

The Quest for Christa T., Christa Wolf, Farrar, Straus and Giroux, Inc.

The Treasury of Knowledge, Jamgon Kongtrul The Great, a Buddhist text currently being translated into English.

Yolanda Van Dyck was born in Scotland and has lived in Nigeria, Trinidad and Holland. She studied biology at the University of Calgary before attending the Alberta College of Art where she graduated with honours in 1978 and then went on to post-graduate studies at the Banff Centre. She has returned over the past years as an Artist-in-Residence at the Leighton Artist Colony in Alberta.

She has won numerous awards and has completed many corporate and private commissions. Her work has been exhibited in Canada, the United States and Europe.

She has been a full-time artist for 20 years and sees her work as a continuum of the tradition of painting as exemplified in the works of Matisse, Dufy and O'Keefe. Ms. Van Dyck currently lives in Calgary with her dog, Kobo. She is represented by Masters Gallery in Calgary.

Betsy Warland has written several books of poetry and
two plays, including the script version of *The Bat Had
Blue Eyes.* Her most recent books include a collection of
prose and essays, *Proper Deafintions, and Two Women in
a Birth,* a collection of her collaborative writing with
Daphne Marlatt. She edited *In Versions — Writing by
Dykes, Queers Lesbians* and lives on a sea mountain
island off the coast of British Columbia.